THE QUICK AND EASY

GIANT DAHLIA QUILT

ON THE SEWING MACHINE

Step-by-Step Instructions and Full-Size Templates for Four Quilt Sizes

Susan Aylsworth Murwin & Suzzy Chalfant Payne

Dover Publications, Inc., New York

To Our Husbands:
Thad R. Murwin and C. Keith Payne

All quilts shown on the covers of this book
designed, machine-pieced and marked for quilting by the authors
and hand-quilted by Bertha Rush.

Published in Canada by General Publishing Company, Ltd., 30 Lesmill Road, Don Mills, Toronto, Ontario.
Published in the United Kingdom by Constable and Company, Ltd., 10 Orange Street, London WC2H 7EG.

The Quick and Easy Giant Dahlia Quilt on the Sewing Machine is a new work, first published by Dover Publications, Inc., in 1983.

Book design by Barbara Effron

Manufactured in the United States of America
Dover Publications, Inc., 31 East 2nd Street, Mineola, N.Y. 11501

Library of Congress Cataloging in Publication Data

Murwin, Susan Aylsworth.
  The quick and easy giant dahlia quilt on the sewing machine.

  1. Quilting. I. Payne, Suzzy Chalfant. II. Title.
TT835.M86   1983   746.9'7041   82-18287
ISBN 0-486-24501-2

CONTENTS

INTRODUCTION

The "Giant Dahlia" is not a traditional patchwork pattern. It was designed in this century. The earliest known appearance of the "Giant Dahlia" was in the 1935 issue of *Needlecraft—The Home Arts Magazine,* published in Augusta, Maine; the original designer is unknown. Our interest in the pattern began when we saw a "Giant Dahlia" quilt at the Mennonite Relief Sale in Harrisburg, Pennsylvania in the late 1970's. At the time we were working on our book, *Creative American Quilting Inspired by the Bible* (Fleming H. Revell, 1983), and we were not free to begin a new project. But we were immediately intrigued by the pattern, and we resolved to attempt it one day.

A few years before, our quilting hobby had become our profession. In the beginning, we certainly never dreamed we would become patchwork and quilting teachers, and then writers about the craft, but it has become our great privilege to have been given this vocation, as teachers of new tricks for an old craft.

Our basic patchwork and quilting classes cover the material in our first book, *Quick and Easy Patchwork on the Sewing Machine* (Dover Publications, 1979), with detailed instructions for all the basic geometric forms as they appear in the major patchwork patterns. Our advanced classes explore combinations of the more complex geometric forms in such patterns as the "Double Wedding Ring," "Hosanna" and "Blazing Star." Both courses have seven class sessions in six weeks, and the students make a complete sampler quilt top of 16 to 30 blocks in that time. Now we teach classes on the "Giant Dahlia" quilt pattern. We meet every other week for three class sessions, and our students bring their completed "Giant Dahlia" quilt tops to the last class.

As soon as the Revell book went to press we began the major task for the "Dahlia" quilt pattern—the drafting. There was no question; it had to be done, and it could not be drawn with yardstick and string. Rather, the nature of the pattern required precision tools for a precision draft. The templates circulating in a few Eastern states were traced on grocery bags or newspapers, and were inevitably inaccurate. Even these templates seemed to be available in only one size quilt. We envisioned all sizes: wall hangings, baby quilts and coverlets, as well as bed-size quilts.

Once we had the templates, we had to figure out how to sew the "Giant Dahlia." There are a number of possible methods, any of which will make a "Dahlia." We tried them all. The sewing instructions in this book are a compilation of many trials and, in our best judgment, the easiest way to piece the pattern. It looks so difficult, but in fact, it is not hard at all to sew. The "Giant Dahlia" builds on the techniques we developed in our basic patchwork book, *Quick and Easy Patchwork on the Sewing Machine.*

The great surprise to us was how ready we were for this pattern, and our students have had the same experience. What excitement to discover that making 16 points meet perfectly in a joint is only an expansion of our earlier directions for the "Eight-Pointed Star." We also found that our tricks for curves (presented first in our instructions for the "Drunkard's Path" pattern) are universal principles, guaranteeing success for even the "Dahlia's" perfect circle.

As never before in our craft, we and our students are finding that we can fulfill that deeply felt need to express ourselves in the medium of American patchwork. We can leap over the technical problems and spend our time and attention on the vastly more pleasurable business of playing with color and design. Indeed, the "Giant Dahlia" quilt pattern is truly satisfying to study and sew.

DESIGNING A "GIANT DAHLIA" QUILT

This pattern looks exactly like its name. The dahlia is a flower. The "Giant Dahlia" is a center-medallion quilt, which simply means that the pattern (in this case, the dahlia) is in the center and extends over the entire quilt. It is similar in concept to the traditional "Lone Star" or "Sunburst" designs, but in contrast to these patterns, all of the angles are replaced by curves. Throughout this book, the center medallion (as opposed to the border; see next paragraph) will be referred to simply as "the medallion." This will avoid confusion with other necessary references to "centers."

A medallion quilt is often enclosed by an elaborate border, and the central flower in the "Giant Dahlia" quilt is certainly enhanced by its decorative border. The sense of the dahlia flower continues into the border petals, but in a stylistic, rather than a realistic fashion.

The goal for any creator of a "Giant Dahlia" quilt is to preserve the portrayal of its flower namesake. There really is no point in coloring this quilt to look like a perfectly round interstellar space body; for this reason, it is important to be aware of the distinct differences in size and shape among the petals. We urge you to spend some time analyzing the basic "Dahlia" design and noting especially the different proportions of the petals. The Color Plan Chart on the next page, showing four petal-arms, will also help you to discern the different petals and to understand how they relate to each other.

As you plan your quilt, ask yourself repeatedly: Is this row of petals clear? Does this petal stand out, or does it blur into the next petal? Does my "Dahlia" look like a dahlia?

We have found that it helps to be aware of some danger spots in the design itself. For example, three petals should be the same color and fabric as the background material used for the "J" corners. These are petals "I" in the medallion and petals "K" and "N" in the border. If these three petals are colored differently from the "J" background, the depiction of a dahlia is lost in both medallion and border. Conversely, petals "G" and "H" on the outside of the medallion should contrast sharply to the "J" background fabric. Following these two guidelines alone will make your "Dahlia" bloom as it should.

The smallest petal in the pattern is "B." Consequently, we think it deserves special treatment. Sometimes this tiny petal can be the secret to an exciting "Giant Dahlia" quilt. Perhaps you will dare to use a color or a shade here that you would not think of using in a larger amount. After selecting this special fabric, check yourself: if you find that you want to repeat this fabric again, maybe the fabric is not rousing enough, so try another. Also, don't forget white! White is bright, and maybe that is all you need for petal "B." Of course, any petal is brilliant only in relationship to the petals on either side of it. The color values of petals "A" and "C" must be dissimilar to even the most unusual petal "B."

The largest petals in the "Dahlia" are "F" and "G." The colors you choose for these petals will tend to dominate your quilt. Be sure that you are satisfied with the effect they will produce.

Is it possible to alternate fabrics in the same row of petals? Yes, if you have basically the same color value in the two fabrics. Otherwise, the row will not be uniform and may jar irregularly and unattractively into the rows around it. Color and color value, then, are probably your most important tools in planning a successful "Giant Dahlia" quilt.

A wide variety of scales (types and sizes) of prints is also desirable. It is not essential, but it helps to choose two or three solid-colored fabrics for certain rows. They will act as dividing lines between the rows of printed fabrics, thus separating the prints so that they do not disappear into each other. "Solid substitutes," which are tiny prints or dots, can replace one or more true solids, if you wish.

You may want to center a specific print design in a particular row of petals, and petals "C" through "G" are the most suitable for this treatment. Using solid colors in the petals on both sides of this row will give it special attention.

A warning about petal "A": it is so narrow and oddly shaped that a solid color or a small print seems to work best.

We tell our students to start with a "main print" or a "main fabric," which is a print or solid color that they fall in love with and just have to have in their quilt. Choose this "main fabric" first, and let it control the quilt. It is surprising how swiftly the perfect other materials appear, once the "main fabric" is selected.

In general, you will probably find it is easiest to work with six to eight fabrics. Four or five just do not seem to be enough to say something interesting, but nine or more may only create confusion.

The border of the "Giant Dahlia" should repeat at least one fabric from the "Dahlia" medallion. As the border is the final statement on any quilt, it should also be an asset. The "M" border petals are collected into groups of four on the straight edge of the "Giant Dahlia" border and into half-circles of eight petals in the corners. The distinct shape of these petals shows up best when a solid color fabric is used.

If your "J" background fabric is light, plan a dark border. If your "J" background is dark, plan a light, bright border. Be careful of having two very different color values in the "Giant Dahlia" border—for example, very light "K" petals and very dark "L" petals. One or the other is likely to vanish!

It seems that we have listed a lot of rules and a lot of "do's" and "don'ts" about the "Giant Dahlia." This has become a joke in our classes. In retaliation for our stern warnings about lost petals and fading flowers, our students will chant to us in singsong style: "Beware of the dreaded petal disappearance!"

Recognize the limits of the pattern, as described above, but let your imagination be in charge as well. We have had students explore the relativity of color and make sophisticated dahlias in shades of white or black! Plan a "Dahlia" in all solids, or try a dark background. The pictures of "Giant Dahlia" quilts on the covers of this book should be helpful.

Finally, we all have to stop planning and begin sewing. Use the Color Plan Chart on this page as a reference guide for placing your colors. Either paste swatches of your fabrics on the chart, or color the petals to represent your fabrics. This prevents mix-ups when sewing.

We see unique benefits in the "Giant Dahlia" quilt pattern. It is a modern design and suits contemporary homes, but it is also stunning in a traditional setting. Perhaps best of all, in contrast to many quilt patterns, it takes amazingly little time to piece the entire "Giant Dahlia" quilt top. The color fantasies of our dreams can be realized so quickly that we can begin again . . . and again.

Color Plan Chart

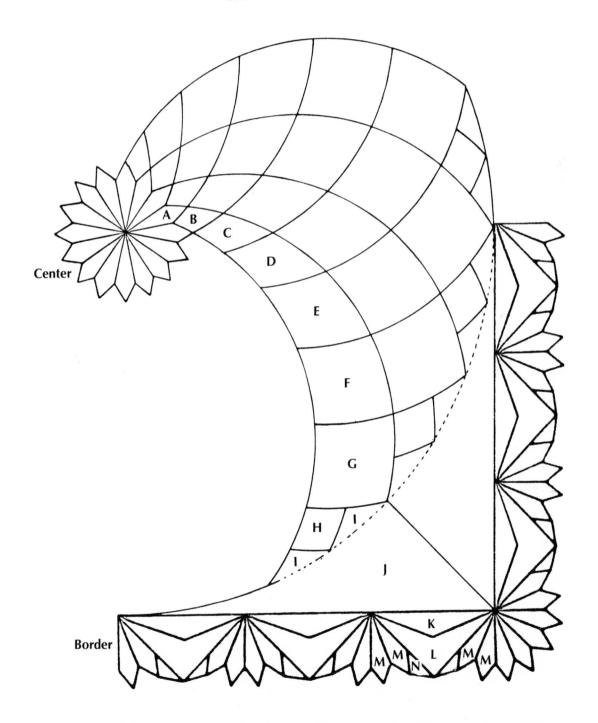

TECHNIQUES FOR MACHINE PIECING

Quilt Sizes

The "Giant Dahlia" quilt pattern is a natural square, but with an extension it can be adapted to a rectangular (oblong) shape. In this book we show three square quilts: 47″ × 47″ finished, 64″ × 64″ finished and 76″ × 76″ finished. A rectangle-extension "Giant Dahlia," 76″ × 98″ finished, is also included as a fourth possibility. The 47″ × 47″ quilt has a 39″ medallion; all the others use the 54″ medallion. In the template section of this book, there are separate pieces for these two different medallion sizes, as well as for the extensions and the borders.

The smallest quilt makes a lovely crib quilt or wall hanging. The 64″ × 64″ "Dahlia" is to be used on top of a spread on a double or queen-size bed. The 76″ × 76″ "Dahlia" is a coverlet for a double bed, while the 76″ × 98″ extension "Dahlia" is a full spread for a double bed or a coverlet for a queen-size bed.

Templates

All of the pattern pieces include the ¼″ seam allowance. They are given in actual-size templates printed on heavyweight paper in the template section of this book. Locate the designated template and cut around the template freehand. For the larger templates that have been divided to fit full-size in this book, cut out the template pieces then tape together, carefully matching the dot/dash lines and letters. With rubber cement, glue the template onto heavy cardboard, such as a medium-weight illustration board or mat board. Then cut precisely on the template cutting lines. Use sandpaper to smooth any rough edges.

Fabrics

Fabrics that are 100% cotton are the most satisfactory. Polyester-cotton blends will work if they feel like cotton. Fabrics with a silky feeling or with a loose weave will not feed smoothly under the pressure foot of the sewing machine. This will cause seam edges to slip, and then your angles, joints and curves will not match accurately.

We strongly suggest that you wash all of your fabrics before cutting out the pattern pieces for your quilt.

Refer to the Yardage Chart on page 14 for the exact fabric yardage requirements for your chosen quilt size.

Illustrations

There are many step-by-step construction drawings throughout the book. These illustrations usually do not indicate specific fabrics. However, the wrong side of the fabric is always shaded; see *Diagram 1*.

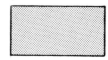

Diagram 1: **The wrong side of the fabric is always shaded.**

Sewing Machine

Use a #11 American-made sewing-machine needle or a #10 European-made sewing-machine needle. Change to a new needle from time to time to ensure smooth sewing.

A stitch length equal to 12 stitches-to-the-inch is recommended. Begin every seam with the needle down in the machine and with the bobbin and needle threads held back out of the way.

Choose a thread in a neutral color. Cotton-covered polyester works best.

Seam Allowance

Use a ¼″ seam allowance on all seams; see *Diagram 2*. Use whatever method is convenient for you, but it is essential to have a dependable method of following the ¼″ seam allowance on your sewing machine.

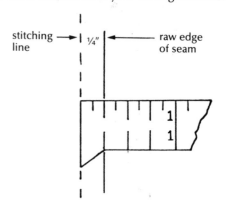

Diagram 2: **The ¼″ seam allowance, measured from the center of the stitching line to the raw edge of the seam.**

A ¼″ seam allowance on all seams is more important for the "Giant Dahlia" quilt pattern than for any other patchwork pattern. This pattern is a perfect circle, and the 360 degrees must be maintained exactly in order for the quilt to lie flat.

In general, seam allowances should be pressed to one side and not opened.

Layered Cutting

Straighten the grain of the fabric. Fold the fabric length-wise, wrong sides together as it comes off the bolt. Turn the folded edge to meet the selvage edges, making four layers. For some smaller templates, you can fold the fabric again to make eight layers.

Grain lines are indicated on each template. Lay the template on the lengthwise fabric grain (see Note below), and trace the outline of the template onto the fabric; see *Diagram 3*. Pin the layers in a few places. Keep fabric flat and carefully cut along your marking lines, as you would cut a dress pattern.

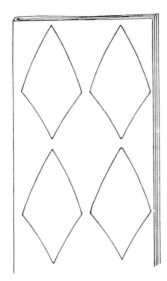

Diagram 3: Example showing tracing lines for the "D" petal of the 54"-medallion "Giant Dahlia," on 44" width fabric folded into 4 layers.

NOTE: We believe all of the petals and border petals of a "Giant Dahlia" quilt should be cut on the lengthwise grain, which runs parallel to the selvages of the fabric. We realize this will require more fabric with some petal shapes, but we have allowed for this in the Yardage Chart on page 14.

Setting In

"Setting in" is necessary whenever angled pieces are being inserted and the design of the block prohibits sewing across seam allowances. The seam allowances at the corner of any "set in" seam are free and will fan in any direction. Seams that begin or end with "setting in" must be locked by one of the methods described below.

Back-Stitch Method: Drop the sewing machine needle into the pieces that are being seamed, exactly ¼" from both raw edges. Lock this seam by sewing forward two stitches, then back-stitching two stitches. Sew forward to the end of the seam. See *Diagram 4.*

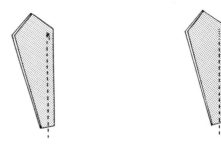

Diagram 4: Back-stitch method.

Diagram 5: Fine-stitch method.

Fine-Stitch Method: The beginning of the "set in" seam can also be locked by changing the stitch length to "fine," sewing a few stitches, then returning the stitch to its customary size for the remainder of the seam. See *Diagram 5.*

Chainsewing Small Units

When combining the pieces of all the small units required to complete a large unit (such as sewing the "M" petals together in the border unit) simply fit these pieces right sides together and feed all the needed units through the sewing machine, assembly-line fashion, so that an approximate 1" chain connects each unit; see *Diagram 6.* Cut the chains to separate the units, and proceed with the pattern instructions.

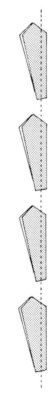

Diagram 6: Sew the pieces together, assembly-line fashion, leaving a 1" chain between units.

Offset Seams

Every seam in the petal-arm unit is offset by ¼" at the beginning and ending of the seam. When patches are offset correctly, the tails of the two pieces will form a "V" and the sewing-machine needle will fall in the center of that "V"; see *Diagram 7*.

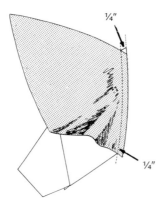

Diagram 7: **The tails of two offset pieces will form a "V" and the sewing-machine needle will fall in the center of that "V."**

The length and shape of the overhanging tails in an offset seam will vary according to the shape and size of the patch. However, the measurement from the inner point of the "V" to the raw edge of the seam allowance is always ¼".

Chainsewing Offset Seams

For extra speed and convenience, the petal-arms may be sewn in chains; see *Diagram 8*.

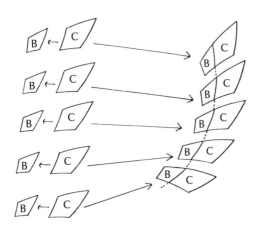

Diagram 8: **"B" petals joined to "C" petals, making a chain of "B-C" petal units.**

Every seam in the petal-arm is an offset seam. This will not be a problem in chainsewing if care is taken to regulate the chains to 1" in length. If a chain is too short it is difficult to correctly maneuver the tails of the offset seam allowance. However, if the chains exceed 1", it is easy for the many petals to become entangled as the petal-arms grow.

Arrange the offsets of a "B-C" unit correctly; see *Offset Seams*, left. Pin, and sew to the end of the seam. Continue sewing so that a 1" chain forms. Slide the offset tails of the next "B-C" unit under the pressure foot so that they are caught by the action of the sewing machine and the needle falls into the center of the "V" tails. Sew to the end of the seam.

Repeat the process for the remaining 14 "B-C" units.

Remove the pins. Open the "C" petals. Add a "D" petal to each "B-C" petal unit; see *Diagram 9*.

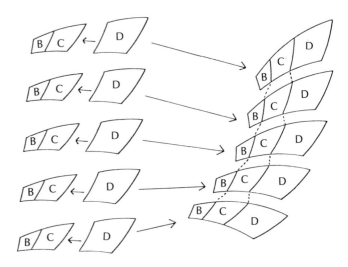

Diagram 9: **"D" petals added to "B-C" petal units, making a chain of "B-C-D" petal units.**

Continue adding the other petals until all 16 petal-arm units are complete, "B" through "I-H-I."

Clip the chains to separate the 16 petal-arms and proceed with the pattern instructions for assembling the "Giant Dahlia."

Seam Joints

Butting Seams: When four or more fabrics meet in a seam, fit the fabric units right sides together and fold back the top edge of the seam allowance so you can see the seam joint on the inside. "Butt" the vertical seam allowances of the center of the joints of the matching units against each other perfectly. Finger press and pin the center seam allowance of the joint on one fabric unit in one direction and the center seam allowance of the joint on the matching fabric unit in the opposite direction; see *Diagram 10*. Pin only through the vertical, center seam allowances, not through the seam joint itself.

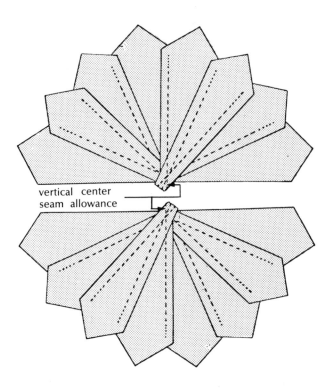

vertical center
seam allowance

Diagram 10: Preparing to "butt" the vertical center seam joint of the "Giant Dahlia" center.

A correctly "butted" seam joint will feel flat, without ridges or bumps.

For perfectly matched joints, it is more important to have the center seam allowances go in opposite directions than to have the seam allowances go toward the darker fabric.

"X" Joint: In a correctly sewn "X" joint, the four petals forming the petal joint cross in a perfect "X"; see *Diagram 11*. The petals just touch at the juncture of the "X" and do not gap at the joint or overlap each other. As in "butted" seams, the vertical seam allowances at each joint go in opposite directions.

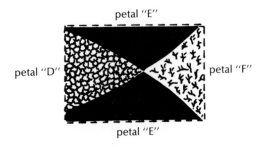

petal "E"

petal "D"   petal "F"

petal "E"

Diagram 11: A close-up illustration of an "X" joint (the "D-E-E-F" joint) in fabric.

NOTE: In the "Giant Dahlia" quilt pattern, the seam allow-ances will automatically go in opposite directions at each

"X" joint because of the pressing directions for each petal-arm on page 20, and the alternating arm instruc-tions on page 21.

Stitching Through the "V's"

When geometric forms with acute angles (such as trian-gles, diamonds, "Giant Dahlia" petals, etc.) meet in 4 to 16 points, have the stitching lines of one full geometric form face up as you sew so you can stitch through the inverted "V" (Λ).

Hold Pin Technique

When geometric forms with acute angles (such as trian-gles, diamonds, "Giant Dahlia" petals, etc.) meet in 4 to 16 points in a long seam, align the exact centers of the two halves right sides together and "butt" seams as de-scribed above. Insert a "hold pin" through the Λ of the visible triangle, diamond, "Giant Dahlia" petal, etc., being sure it emerges precisely through the Λ of the visi-ble geometric form on the back, and that it holds the two halves level; see *Diagram 12*.

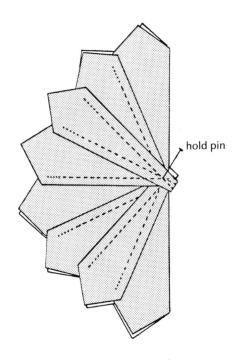

hold pin

Diagram 12: Right sides together, "butt" the center seam and insert a "hold pin" through the "Λ."

Finger press the vertical, center seam allowances in opposite directions and pin both; see *Diagram 13*. Re-move the "hold pin." Stitch the seam; see *Diagram 14*.

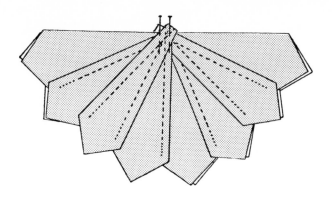

Diagram 13: **Pin seam allowances of the center seam in opposite directions. Remove the "hold pin."**

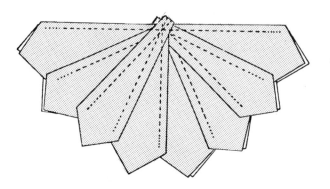

Diagram 14: **A correctly sewn seam.**

Sewing Curves

When sewing curves, always have the patch with the concave curve on top, because you are easing this to fit the convex patch (which is on the bottom); see *Diagram 15.*

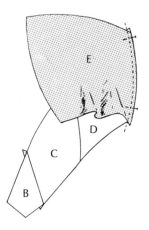

Diagram 15: **Example showing "E" petal being eased to fit "D" petal of the "B-C-D" unit.**

Pressing Instructions

All raw edges of the "Giant Dahlia" and most border edges are cut on the bias.

Use a warm setting and a dry iron for all unit pressing in order to avoid stretching or distorting the fabrics as you construct the center, petal-arms and borders of the "Dahlia."

The completed "Dahlia" medallion may be pressed with a steam setting.

Invisible Appliqué Stitch

The invisible appliqué stitch is a running stitch on the back of the base fabric, and a running stitch in the crease of the fold of the piece being appliquéd. Both the running stitch on the base and the running stitch in the crease of the fold of the top piece are the same length. When done correctly, both stitches are invisible on the front.

Use a single thread with a knot. Bring the needle and thread through the base fabric, from back to front (*Detail A*). Take a small stitch in the crease formed by the fold of the top piece (*Detail B*), then gently tug the thread to complete the stitch (*Detail C*). Insert the point of the needle into the base, exactly *behind* the spot where the thread emerged in the fold and *below* the level of the top fold (*Detail D*). Take another running stitch in the base, then a running stitch in the fold on the top piece, and so forth. Every three or four stitches, gently tug the thread, and all the stitches will disappear. See *Details E* and *F* for other views of this stitch.

- Never angle your stitch, or the thread will show like a hemming stitch.

- Never have fabrics of both base and top on the needle at the same time, or your stitches will show like a hemming stitch.

- Be sure the running stitches on the back of the base fabric, and the running stitches in the crease of the fold of the appliquéd fabric, are the *same length*. This ensures the strength of the "invisible appliqué stitch," as well as its invisibility. The ideal stitch length is about two millimeters, a little less than one eighth of an inch.

- Use commercial quilting thread, which is stronger than polyester-cotton thread and is coated to prevent knotting.

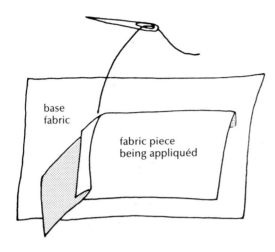

Detail A: Use a single thread with a knot; insert the needle and thread through the base fabric only, from back to front.

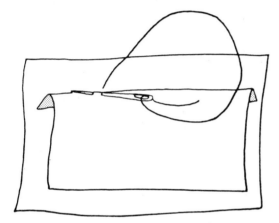

Detail B: Take a small stitch in the crease formed by the fold of the piece being appliquéd. Note that the point of the needle is inserted into the crease precisely in front of the thread that has emerged from the base fabric.

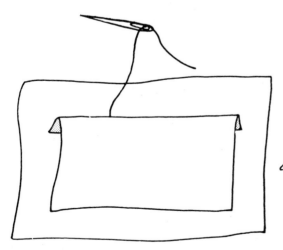

Detail C: Pull the needle and thread through to complete the stitch in the crease of the fold.

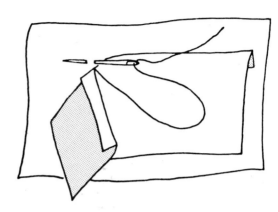

Detail D: Next, take a stitch in the base fabric, inserting the point of the needle into the backing fabric exactly *behind* the spot where the thread emerged from the fold, and slightly *below* the level of that fold.

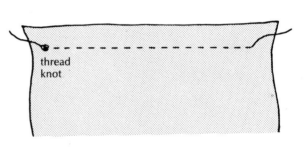

Detail E: Illustration of a completed row of invisible appliqué running stitches viewed from the wrong side of the base fabric.

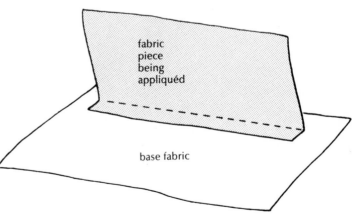

Detail F: The running stitches of the invisible appliqué stitch inside the crease formed by the fold are the same length as the running stitches on the wrong side of the base fabric.

"GIANT DAHLIA" QUILT YARDAGE CHART

Finished Quilt Size	47" × 47"	64" × 64"	76" × 76"	76" × 98"
	39" center	54" center	54" center	54" center
cut 16	A = 1/4 yd.	A = 1/4 yd.	A = 1/4 yd.	A = 1/4 yd.
cut 16	B = 1/4 yd.	B = 1/4 yd.	B = 1/4 yd.	B = 1/4 yd.
cut 16	C = 1/4 yd.	C = 1/2 yd.	C = 1/2 yd.	C = 1/2 yd.
cut 16	D = 3/8 yd.	D = 5/8 yd.	D = 5/8 yd.	D = 5/8 yd.
cut 16	E = 1/2 yd.	E = 3/4 yd.	E = 3/4 yd.	E = 3/4 yd.
cut 16	F = 5/8 yd.	F = 1 yd.	F = 1 yd.	F = 1 yd.
cut 16	G = 5/8 yd.	G = 1 yd.	G = 1 yd.	G = 1 yd.
cut 16	H = 1/4 yd.	H = 3/8 yd.	H = 3/8 yd.	H = 3/8 yd.
cut 32	I = 3/8 yd.	I = 3/8 yd.	I = 3/8 yd.	I = 3/8 yd.
cut 8	*J = 5/8 yd.	*J = 7/8 yd.	*J = 3 1/4 yds.	*J = 5 yds. (includes 22 1/2" × 66 1/2"-long strip)
	Border	**Border**	**Border**	**Border**
cut 24	K = 1/2 yd.	K = 3/4 yd.	K = 7/8 yd.	K = 7/8 yd.
cut 24	L = 1/2 yd.	L = 3/4 yd.	L = 7/8 yd.	L = 1 1/8 yds.
cut 112	M = 3/4 yd.	M = 1 3/8 yds.	M = 1 3/4 yds.	M = 1 3/4 yds.
cut 48	N = 1/4 yd.	N = 3/8 yd.	N = 3/8 yd.	N = 3/8 yd.
	Backing & Binding	**Backing & Binding**	**Backing & Binding**	**Backing & Binding**
	3 7/8 yds.	4 7/8 yds.	5 3/4 yds.	7 1/8 yds.

* The fabric for the "J" template should be folded lengthwise into four layers. The "J" template is an asymmetrical figure, having a right and a left side. This is not a problem for the layered method of cutting because half of the layers of material within each folded length of fabric are right side up and half are wrong side up.

THE QUICK AND EASY

GIANT
DAHLIA
QUILT

ON THE SEWING MACHINE

DIRECTIONS FOR SEWING THE "GIANT DAHLIA" MEDALLION (BOTH SIZES)

Diagram 16: The "Giant Dahlia" quilt and borders—39"-medallion and 54"-medallion.

Construction of the Center of the Medallion

The templates used to make the center of the 39″-medallion "Giant Dahlia" are on Plates 1–4, 6–7. Those for the 54″-medallion are on Plates 6–13. We will begin by constructing the centers of these two size medallions; see *Diagram 16*.

The template used to make the center of the 39″ medallion is template "A" on Plate 1. The template used to make the center of the 54″ medallion is template "A" on Plate 7. See *Diagram 17*. In the following discussion, "template 'A' " will refer to the appropriate one for the size you are making.

Diagram 17: Center of the "Giant Dahlia" medallion; make one.

1. Layer-cut 16 template "A" pieces; see *Layered Cutting* on page 9.

2. Assemble the four quarters of the center (see *Diagram 18*) according to the following instructions and diagrams.

Diagram 18: Quarter unit of the "Giant Dahlia" center; make four.

(a) Sew "A" petal #1 to "A" petal #2, beginning at the outside edge, and "setting in" ¼"; see *Diagram 19*. Sew to the end of the seam. Open. See *Setting In* on page 9.
(b) Add "A" petal #3, "setting in" ¼". Sew to the end of the seam; finger press the seam allowance of "A" petals #1 and #2 to your left as you sew across it. Open.

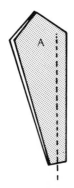

Diagram 19: Sew "A" petals together, "setting in" ¼".

(c) Add "A" petal #4, "setting in" ¼". Sew to the end of the seam; finger press the seam allowance of "A" petals #2 and #3 to your left as you sew across it. Open.
(d) The third seam allowance will fall to the right naturally, so that all stitching lines of "A" petal #3 will be visible on the back; see *Diagram 20*.
(e) Repeat the above instructions, making three additional units.

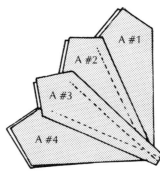

Diagram 20: All stitching lines of "A" petal #3 will be visible on the back.

3. Join two quarters of the "Dahlia" center; see *Diagram 21*. "Set in" ¼" and sew to the end of the seam; see *Diagram 22*. See *Stitching Through the "V's"* on page 11 and *Hold Pin Technique* on page 11.

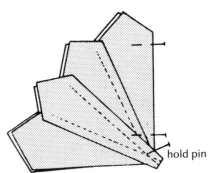

hold pin

Diagram 21: Pin two quarters of the center together, inserting a "hold pin" at the "Λ" on petal #3.

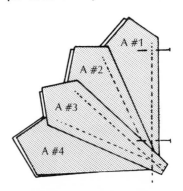

Diagram 22: The correctly sewn seam goes exactly through the "Λ" formed by the stitching lines of petal #3.

4. Repeat the instructions given in Step 3, making the bottom half of the center of the "Giant Dahlia"; see *Diagram 23.*

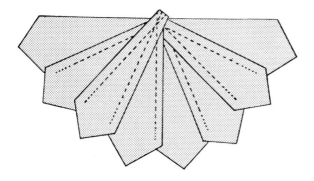

Diagram 23: **Bottom half of the center, opened.**

5. Join the top and bottom halves of the "Dahlia" center, "setting in" ¼" at the beginning and at the end of this center seam; see *Diagram 24.* Open. This center seam allowance may be pressed to one side or it may be pressed open; choose the method that works best with your fabrics. See *Butting Seams* on page 10, *Stitching through the "V's"* on page 11 and *Hold Pin Technique* on page 11.

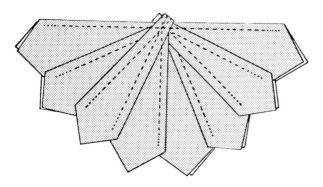

Diagram 24: **Stitch the top and bottom halves of the center together.**

Construction of the Petal-Arms

All 16 petal-arms should curve to the right; see *Diagram 25.* Every seam in the petal-arm unit is an offset seam. See *Offset Seams* on page 10. For extra speed and convenience the petal-arms may be sewn in chains. See *Chainsewing Offset Seams* on page 10.

The eight petal templates used to make the petal-arms of the 39"-medallion "Giant Dahlia" appear on

Plates 1 through 3. The eight templates used to make the petal-arms of the 54"-medallion "Giant Dahlia" appear on Plates 6 through 11. In both cases, they are called templates "B" through "I."

1. Layer-cut the following pieces; see *Layered Cutting* on page 9.

> Template "B"—cut 16
> Template "C"—cut 16
> Template "D"—cut 16
> Template "E"—cut 16
> Template "F"—cut 16
> Template "G"—cut 16
> Template "H"—cut 16
> Template "I"—cut 32

2. Sew petal "B" to petal "C"; see *Diagram 26.* This is a straight seam, but all seam edges are on the bias. Handle your fabric pieces with care to avoid stretching the edges. Two or three pins should be sufficient for every seam, however.
(a) Position petal "C" over petal "B," "offset" by the ¼" seam allowance at the beginning and at the end of the seam.
(b) Pin each end of the seam. Sew and ease to fit. See *Offset Seams* on page 10.
(c) Sew the remaining "B-C" units. Remove pins. Open "C" petals.

3. Sew petal "D" to "B-C" unit; see *Diagram 27.* From this point in the construction of the petal-arm, all the seams are curved seams; see *Sewing Curves* on page 12.
(a) Position petal "D" over petal "C," "offset" by the ¼" seam allowance at the beginning and at the end of the seam.
(b) Pin each end of the seam. Sew and ease to fit.
(c) Sew the remaining "B-C-D" units. Remove pins. Open "D" petals.

4. Sew petal "E" to "B-C-D" unit; see *Diagram 28.*
(a) Position petal "E" over petal "D," "offset" by the ¼" seam allowance at the beginning and at the end of the seam.
(b) Pin each end of the seam. Sew and ease to fit.
(c) Sew the remaining "B-C-D-E" units. Remove pins. Open "E" petals.

5. Sew petal "F" to "B-C-D-E" unit; see *Diagram 29.*
(a) Position petal "F" over petal "E," "offset" by the ¼" seam allowance at the beginning and at the end of the seam.
(b) Pin each end of the seam. Sew and ease to fit.
(c) Sew the remaining "B-C-D-E-F" units. Remove pins. Open "F" petals.

6. Sew petal "G" to "B-C-D-E-F" unit; see *Diagram 30.*
(a) Position petal "G" over petal "F," "offset" by the ¼" seam allowance at the beginning and at the end of the seam. The tails of petal "G" as it fits over petal "F" are so shallow on both ends that they seem almost flat.
(b) Pin each end of the seam. Sew and ease to fit.
(c) Sew the remaining "B-C-D-E-F-G" units. Remove pins. Open "G" petals.

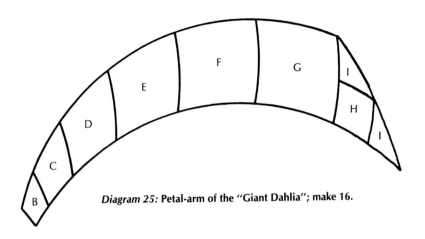

Diagram 25: Petal-arm of the "Giant Dahlia"; make 16.

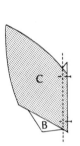

Diagram 26: Pin and sew petal "C" to petal "B," offsetting seam.

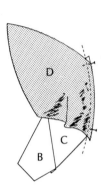

Diagram 27: Pin and sew petal "D" to petal "C," offsetting seam.

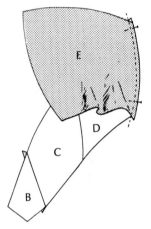

Diagram 28: Pin and sew petal "E" to petal "D," offsetting seam.

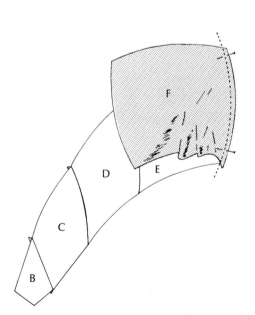

Diagram 29: Pin and sew petal "F" to petal "E," offsetting seam.

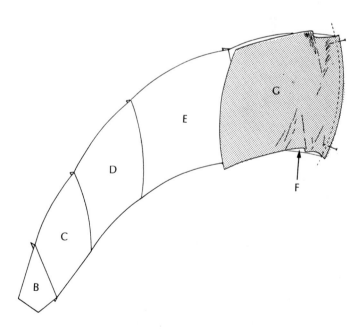

Diagram 30: Pin and sew petal "G" to petal "F," offsetting seam.

7. Sew "I-H-I" units together by adding "I" petals to "H" petal following the numbered order on *Diagram 31*.

(a) Pin petal "I" #1 to petal "H"; see *Diagram 32*. Sew in direction of arrow. Open. Press seam allowance toward "I" petal.

(b) Pin petal "I" #2 over "I-H" unit; see *Diagram 33*. Sew in direction of arrow. Open. Press seam allowance toward "I" #2 petal.

(c) Sew the remaining 15 "I-H-I" units.

8. Sew "I-H-I" unit to petal-arm ("B-C-D-E-F-G" unit); see *Diagram 34*.

(a) Position "I-H-I" unit over petal "G." The beginning of the seam will match exactly. The end of the seam will be a very shallow offset, as shown in *Diagram 34*.

(b) Pin at each end of the seam. Sew and ease to fit. Open.

(c) Add the remaining "I-H-I" units to the remaining petal-arms.

9. Press the petal-arms in two combinations:

(a) Press all seam allowances of one half of the petal-arms (eight) toward "B" petal.

(b) Press all seam allowances of remaining eight petal-arms toward "I-H-I" units.

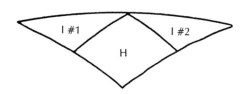

Diagram 31: "I-H-I" unit; make 16.

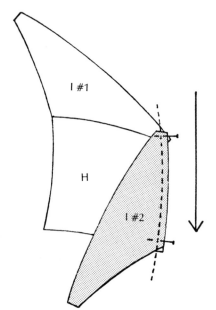

Diagram 33: Pin and sew "I" #2 to "I-H" unit.

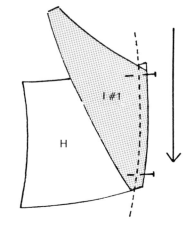

Diagram 32: **Pin and sew "I" #1 petal to "H" petal, offsetting seam.**

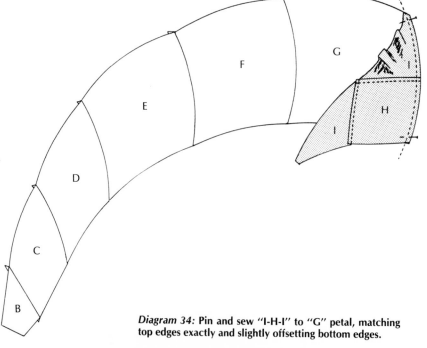

Diagram 34: **Pin and sew "I-H-I" to "G" petal, matching top edges exactly and slightly offsetting bottom edges.**

Sewing the Petal-Arms to the Center of the Medallion

Alternate the petal-arms that have all seam allowances pressed toward "B" petals and the petal-arms that have all seam allowances pressed toward "I-H-I" units.

1. Sew seam #1 (short seam).
(a) Position the center of the medallion over a petal-arm; see *Diagram 35*.
(b) Right sides together, match an "A" petal to "B" end of petal-arm; see *Diagrams 36A and 36B*. "Set in" ¼" at the beginning of the seam. Sew to the end of this short seam, in the direction of the arrow; see *Setting In* on page 9.

2. Sew seam #2 (long seam).
(a) Arrange petal-arm #2 over petal-arm #1, and pin every joint; see *"X" Joint* on page 11. There are six "X" joints in every long petal-arm seam; see *Diagram 37*.
(b) "Set in" ¼" at "A" petal (the beginning of the seam) and sew the entire length of the petal-arm in a continuous seam, easing the concave curve over the convex curve; see *Sewing Curves* on page 12.
3. Sew seam #3 (short seam). Open petal-arm #2 and sew seam #3 (a short seam) like seam #1.
4. Continue adding the other 14 petal-arms to the center of the medallion until the circle of the "Giant Dahlia" is complete.

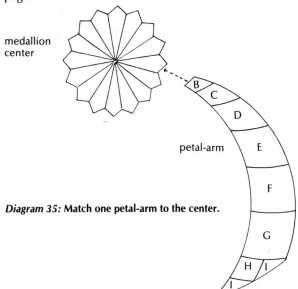

Diagram 35: **Match one petal-arm to the center.**

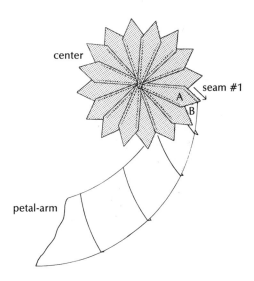

Diagram 36A: **Add the first petal-arm to the center of the 39" medallion and sew seam #1.**

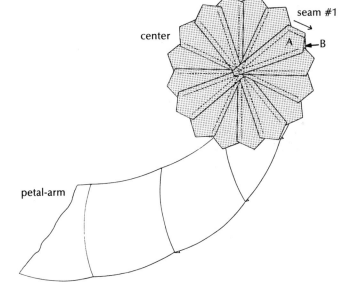

Diagram 36B: **Add the first petal-arm to the center of the 54" medallion and sew seam #1.**

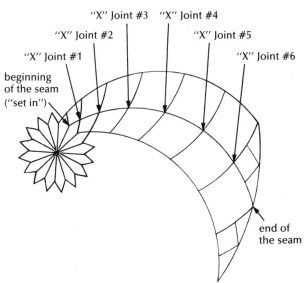

Diagram 37: **Pin and sew petal-arm #2 to petal-arm #1, making six "X" joints.**

Pressing the Finished "Giant Dahlia" Circle

The completed circle of the "Giant Dahlia" should be handled and pressed with care, because the circumference of the "Dahlia" is cut on the bias and can be stretched out of shape easily.

Press the long seams of the petal-arms toward the concave curves. Press the "set in" seams of the "A" petals in the center of the "Giant Dahlia" as they naturally fall.

Constructing the "J" Corners

The template used to make the corners of the 39"-medallion "Giant Dahlia" is template "J" on Plates 6 and 7. The template used to make the corners of the 54"-medallion "Giant Dahlia" is template "J" on Plates 12 and 13. Carefully cut out the template pieces and tape together, matching letters and dot/dash lines.

1. Right sides together, match and sew two "J" corners on the long straight edge, as shown. Sew in the direction of the arrow; see *Diagrams 38* and *39.*

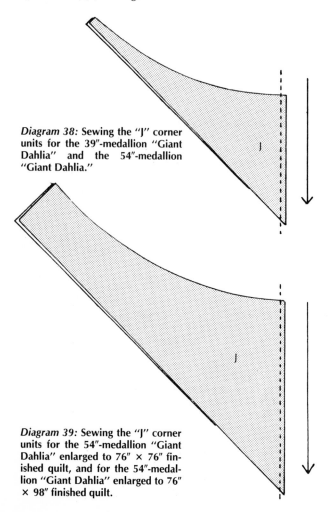

Diagram 38: Sewing the "J" corner units for the 39"-medallion "Giant Dahlia" and the 54"-medallion "Giant Dahlia."

Diagram 39: Sewing the "J" corner units for the 54"-medallion "Giant Dahlia" enlarged to 76" × 76" finished quilt, and for the 54"-medallion "Giant Dahlia" enlarged to 76" × 98" finished quilt.

2. Make three additional "J" corner units.

3. Join narrow ends of "J" corner units until large open circle is complete; see *Diagrams 40* and *41.* Handle carefully; do not stretch this open circle.

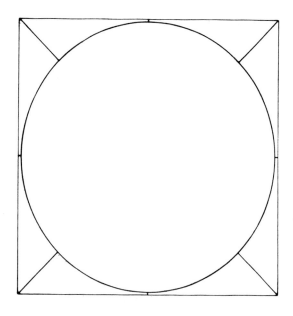

Diagram 40: The frame of "J" corner units for the 39"-medallion "Giant Dahlia" and the 54"-medallion "Giant Dahlia."

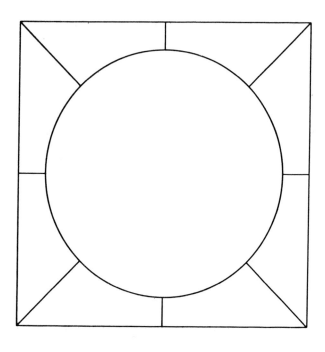

Diagram 41: The frame of "J" corner units for the 54"-medallion "Giant Dahlia" enlarged to 76" × 76" finished quilt and the 54"-medallion "Giant Dahlia" enlarged to 76" × 98" finished quilt.

Joining the Circle of "J" Corners to Completed "Dahlia"

1. Match and pin the long and short seams of the "J" frame to the points of the large "G" petals. Consult the following diagrams for assistance in spacing: See *Diagram 16* on page 16 for the 39"-medallion "Giant Dahlia" and the 54"-medallion "Giant Dahlia." See *Diagram 61* on page 26 for the 54"-medallion "Giant Dahlia" enlarged to 76" × 76" finished quilt. See *Diagram 63* on page 27 for the 54"-medallion "Giant Dahlia" enlarged to 76" × 98" finished quilt.

2. Sew and ease to fit. Press the seam allowance toward the "J" frame.

Border of the "Giant Dahlia"

See *Diagrams 42* and *43*. The four templates used to make the borders of the various quilt sizes are all labeled "K" through "N." Those used to make the border of the 39"-medallion "Giant Dahlia" are found on Plates 3 and 4. Those used to make the border of the 54"-medallion "Giant Dahlia" are found on Plates 9 and 14. Those used to make the border of the 54"-medallion "Giant Dahlia" enlarged to a 76" × 76" finished quilt are found on Plates 15 and 16. The templates on Plates 15 and 16 are also used to make the border of the 54"-medallion "Giant Dahlia" enlarged to a 76" × 98" finished quilt.

Diagram 42: **Border of the "Giant Dahlia" quilt.**

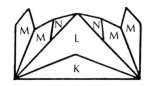

Diagram 43: **Border unit of the "Giant Dahlia"; make 24.**

1. Layer-cut the following pieces; see *Layered Cutting* on page 9.

    Template "K"—cut 24
    Template "L"—cut 24
    Template "M"—cut 112
    Template "N"—cut 48

2. Assemble the four corner units (see *Diagram 44*) of the border of the "Giant Dahlia" according to the following instructions and diagrams.

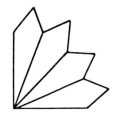

Diagram 44: **Corner unit of the "Giant Dahlia"; make four.**

(a) Sew "M" petal #1 to "M" petal #2, beginning at the outside edge and sewing to the end of the seam; see *Diagram 45*. Open.

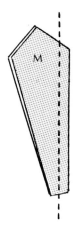

Diagram 45: **Sew "M" petal #1 to "M" petal #2.**

(b) Add "M" petal #3. Sew to the end of the seam. Finger press the seam allowance of "M" petals #1 and #2 to your left as you sew across it. Open.

(c) Add "M" petal #4. Sew to the end of the seam. Finger press the seam allowance of "M" petals #2 and #3 to your left as you sew across it.

23

(d) The third seam allowance will fall to the right naturally, so that all stitching lines of "M" petal #3 will be visible on the back; see *Diagram 46.*

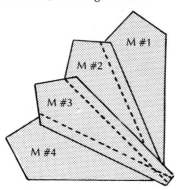

Diagram 46: All stitching lines of "M" petal #3 will be visible on the back.

(e) Repeat the above instructions, making three additional corner units; set corner units aside.

3. Construct the "K-L" units according to the following instructions and diagrams.

(a) Clip all boomerang-shaped "L" pattern pieces as shown on the template.

(b) Position boomerang "L" over large triangle "K" as shown in *Diagram 47,* folding back half of the boomerang at clipped edge. Sew in direction of arrow. When the stitching line reaches the clip at the obtuse angle, release the pressure foot. Pivot the pattern pieces on the sewing-machine needle. Match and pin boomerang "L" over triangle "K" as shown. Drop the pressure foot and sew to the end of the seam; see *Diagram 48.* Open and press the seam allowance toward triangle "K."

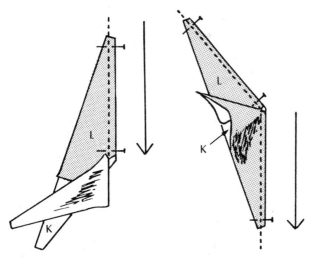

Diagram 47: Pin and stitch "L" to "K," folding back half of "L" at clipped edge.

Diagram 48: Pivot "L"; match and pin to "K," then stitch to end of seam.

4. Construct the "M-M-N" units according to the following instructions and diagrams.

(a) Chainsew all "M" petals in pairs. Clip chains apart. Open. See *Chainsewing Small Units* on page 9.

(b) Add small triangle "N" to "M" petal pairs, "offset" by the ¼" seam allowance, where necessary, making two combinations as shown in *Diagram 49:* side one and side two. See *Offset Seams* on page 10. Sew in direction of arrows. The inside of the "M-M-N" unit is face upward when you sew the side-two combination, as shown in the diagrams.

side one ⟶ ⟵ side two

Diagram 49: Make two combinations of the "M-M-N" units; side one and side two.

NOTE: The angles of the "M" border template for the 39"-medallion "Giant Dahlia" are more acute than the angles of the "M" template of the 54"-medallion "Dahlia" and of the "M" template of the 76" × 76" and 76" × 98" extension "Dahlias." Therefore, the tails of the offset are different when triangle "N" is added. See *Diagrams 50–55* for guidance.

(c) Open. Press both seam allowances of the "M-M-N" unit toward the middle "M" petal.

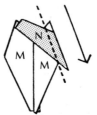

Diagram 50: 39" medallion of the "Dahlia": side one.

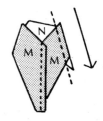

Diagram 51: 39" medallion of the "Dahlia": side two.

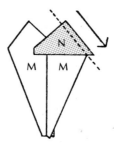

Diagram 52: 54" medallion of the "Dahlia": side one.

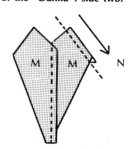

Diagram 53: 54" medallion of the "Dahlia": side two.

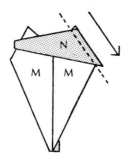

Diagram 54: 76" × 76" extension "Dahlia" and 76" × 98" extension "Dahlia": side one.

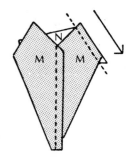

Diagram 55: 76" × 76" extension "Dahlia" and 76" × 98" extension "Dahlia": side two.

5. Add the "M-M-N" units to the "K-L" unit.
(a) Right sides together, position "K-L" unit over side-one "M-M-N" unit; see *Diagram 56*. "Butt" seam allowances at the narrow end of the seam and pin; sew in direction of arrow. See *Butting Seams* on page 10.

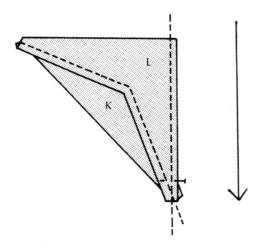

Diagram 56: **Pin and stitch the "K-L" unit over the side-one "M-M-N" unit; although not visible, the right side of the "M-M-N" unit is face upward.**

(b) Open. Press seam allowance toward the "M-M-N" unit.
(c) Right sides together, position side-two "M-M-N" unit over border unit; see *Diagram 57*. "Butt" seam allowances at the narrow end of the seam and pin. Sew in direction of arrow.

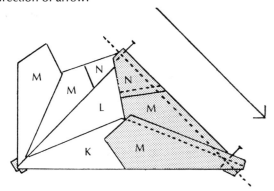

Diagram 57: **Pin and stitch side-two "M-M-N" unit to border unit.**

(d) Open. Press seam allowance toward the "M-M-N" unit; see *Diagram 58*.
(e) Make 23 additional border units.

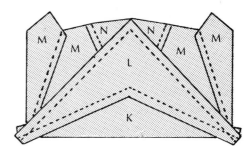

Diagram 58: **Wrong side of border unit showing "K-L" seam allowances pressed toward "M-M-N" units.**

6. Sew border units together in rows of six, making four borders; see *Diagram 59*. See *Butting Seams* on page 10, *Stitching Through the "V's"* on page 11 and *Hold Pin Technique* on page 11. Press seam allowances OPEN.

Diagram 59: **Sew border units together in rows of six.**

7. Add the borders to the "Giant Dahlia" according to the following instructions and diagrams.
(a) Pin and sew a border to the top and a border to the bottom of the "Giant Dahlia." Consult the following diagrams for assistance in spacing: See *Diagram 16* on page 16 for the 39"-medallion "Giant Dahlia" and the 54"-medallion "Giant Dahlia." See *Diagram 61* on page 26 for the 54"-medallion "Giant Dahlia" enlarged to 76" × 76" finished quilt. See *Diagram 63* on page 27 for the 54"-medallion "Giant Dahlia" enlarged to 76" × 98" finished quilt.
(b) Press the border seam allowances toward the "Giant Dahlia."
(c) Add the corner units to the opposite ends of the remaining two borders; see *Diagram 60*.

Diagram 60: **Add corner units to two borders.**

(d) Pin and sew these long borders to the opposite sides of the "Giant Dahlia." See *Butting Seams* on page 10 and *Stitching Through the "V's"* on page 11. Press the border seam allowances toward the "Giant Dahlia."

Enlarging a 54″-Medallion "Dahlia" to a 76″ × 76″ Finished Quilt

The "J" template used to make the 76″ × 76″ extension "Giant Dahlia" (*Diagram 61*) is found on Plates 12 and 13; the border templates ("K" through "N") are found on Plates 15 and 16.

1. Make a 54″-medallion "Dahlia" following the instructions found on pages 16 to 22.

2. Enlarge the "J" corner template according to the following instructions and diagram.

(a) Following cutting lines exactly, cut out the pieces for the 54″-medallion "J" corner template and tape together, matching letters and dot/dash lines.

(b) Using rubber cement, glue the complete "J" corner template onto a large sheet of poster board.

(c) Extend the measurements of the right-angle corner by six inches and draw a new base line for the template, extending the other corner as shown in *Diagram 62*.

(d) Cut out the new "J" corner template.

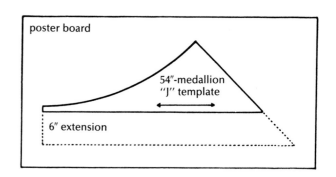

Diagram 62: Add a 6″ extension to the "J" corner template.

(e) Proceed with the instructions on page 23 for adding the "J" corners to the 54″ "Giant Dahlia" medallion.

3. Following the border instructions found on pages 23 to 25, construct the extension border and add to the 54″ "Giant Dahlia" medallion.

Diagram 61: 54″-medallion "Giant Dahlia" enlarged to a 76″ × 76″ finished quilt, including borders.

Enlarging a 54"-Medallion "Dahlia" to a 76" × 98" Finished Quilt

The "J" template used to make the 76" × 98" extension "Giant Dahlia" (*Diagram 63*) is found on Plates 12 and 13; the border templates are found on Plates 15 and 16.

1. Make a 54"-medallion "Dahlia" following the instructions found on pages 16 to 22.

2. Enlarge the "J" corner template according to the following instructions and diagram.

(a) Following cutting lines exactly, cut out the pieces for the 54"-medallion "J" corner template and tape together, matching letters and dot/dash lines.

(b) Using rubber cement, glue the complete "J" corner template onto a large sheet of poster board.

(c) Extend the measurements of the right angle corner by six inches and draw a new base line for the template, extending the other corner as shown in *Diagram 64*.

(d) Cut out the new "J" corner template.

(e) Proceed with the instructions on page 23 for adding the "J" corners to the 54" "Giant Dahlia" medallion.

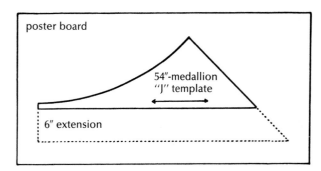

Diagram 64: **Add a 6" extension to the "J" corner template.**

3. Cut or tear a 22½"-wide × 66½"-long strip of cloth the same color as your "J" corner fabric; sew this strip to the top of your quilt.

4. Following the border instructions found on pages 23 to 25, and making four additional border units, construct the extension border and add to the 54" "Giant Dahlia" medallion. See *Diagram 63* for guidance in placing the additional border units on the long sides of the quilt.

Diagram 63: **54"-medallion "Giant Dahlia" enlarged to a 76" × 98" finished quilt, including borders.**

Binding the "Giant Dahlia"

The binding finishes the raw edges of the quilt and encloses these raw edges: quilt top, batting and fabric backing. It should be made from the same fabric used for the backing. Apply the binding to the quilt after the quilt has been quilted and removed from the frame, hoop, etc. Assembly of the quilt (top, batting and lining) and quilting instructions are not covered in this book; refer to the many excellent quilting books currently on the market for this information.

1. Prepare the fabric for binding.
(a) Measure a quilt side, excluding the corner units as shown in *Diagram 65*. This measurement will be approximately:

39" for a 47" × 47" finished "Giant Dahlia"
54" for a 64" × 64" finished "Giant Dahlia"

66" for a 76" × 76" finished "Giant Dahlia"
and
66" for the two short sides, 88" for the two long sides of a 76" × 98" finished "Giant Dahlia"

(b) Add ½" to your measurement to allow for seam allowances.

(c) Four long binding strips are needed for one quilt. Cut the strips on the crosswise or lengthwise grain; if necessary, piece the strips in order to reach the desired length.
    (i) A 2½"-wide strip is needed for a 47" × 47" finished "Giant Dahlia."
    (ii) A 3"-wide strip is needed for a 64" × 64", 76" × 76" or 76" × 98" finished "Giant Dahlia."

(d) Choose the binding corner template "O" that fits your size quilt, and cut four curved corner units for one quilt; clip inside corner as shown on template. The binding corner templates are found on Plates 4 and 5.

Diagram 65: Measuring a quilt side of a 39"-medallion "Giant Dahlia" or a 54"-medallion "Giant Dahlia."

(e) Sew straight binding strips to corner units, completing a frame of binding; see *Diagram 66*.

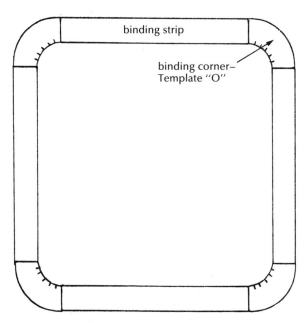

Diagram 66: **Sew straight strips to corners, completing a frame of binding.**

(f) Press under a ¼" hem on the inner edge of the binding, the side with the clipped curve; see *Diagram 67*.

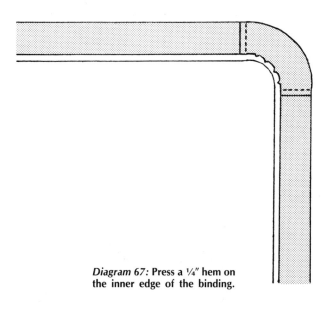

Diagram 67: **Press a ¼" hem on the inner edge of the binding.**

2. Prepare the quilt to receive the binding.
(a) Baste, by hand, the outside edges of the quilt ¼" from the edge of the quilt.
(b) Trim the batting and backing to match the edges of the quilt top.

3. Sew the binding to the quilt.
(a) Right sides together, match quilt to binding. Pin the

quilt to the binding with the wrong side of the quilt toward you as you pin; see *Diagram 68*.
(b) Sew the quilt to the binding with a ¼" seam. Use a short stitch (12 to 15 stitches-to-the-inch). The use of a "Smooth and Even Feed Sewing Machine Foot" attachment will help prevent pulling or puckers.

To turn the quilt at sharp angles, release the pressure foot and pivot the quilt on the sewing-machine needle. Drop the pressure foot, and continue the sewing line in a new direction. Repeat at every angle.
(c) Trim binding and edge of quilt to ⅛".
(d) Clip deep angles; clip away tips of sharp points.
(e) Turn the binding to the back of the quilt. Insert a pointed object under the binding at the sharp angles, and push the border points right side out.
(f) Pin and then sew the binding to the back of the quilt using an "invisible appliqué stitch"; see *Invisible Appliqué Stitch* on pages 12–13.

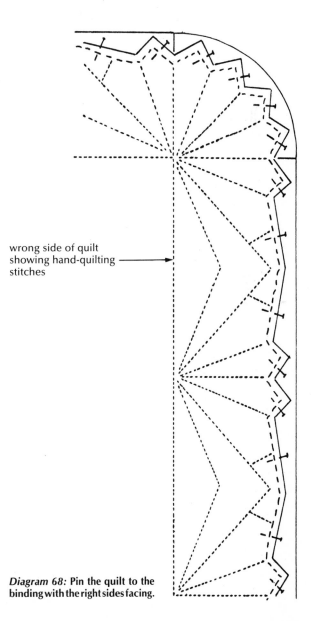

wrong side of quilt showing hand-quilting stitches

Diagram 68: **Pin the quilt to the binding with the right sides facing.**

29

METRIC CONVERSION CHART

CONVERTING INCHES TO CENTIMETERS AND YARDS TO METERS

mm — millimeters   cm — centimeters   m — meters

INCHES INTO MILLIMETERS AND CENTIMETERS
(Slightly rounded off for convenience)

inches	mm		cm	inches	cm	inches	cm	inches	cm
⅛	3mm			5	12.5	21	53.5	38	96.5
¼	6mm			5½	14	22	56	39	99
⅜	10mm	or	1cm	6	15	23	58.5	40	101.5
½	13mm	or	1.3cm	7	18	24	61	41	104
⅝	15mm	or	1.5cm	8	20.5	25	63.5	42	106.5
¾	20mm	or	2cm	9	23	26	66	43	109
⅞	22mm	or	2.2cm	10	25.5	27	68.5	44	112
1	25mm	or	2.5cm	11	28	28	71	45	114.5
1¼	32mm	or	3.2cm	12	30.5	29	73.5	46	117
1½	38mm	or	3.8cm	13	33	30	76	47	119.5
1¾	45mm	or	4.5cm	14	35.5	31	79	48	122
2	50mm	or	5cm	15	38	32	81.5	49	124.5
2½	65mm	or	6.5cm	16	40.5	33	84	50	127
3	75mm	or	7.5cm	17	43	34	86.5		
3½	90mm	or	9cm	18	46	35	89		
4	100mm	or	10cm	19	48.5	36	91.5		
4½	115mm	or	11.5cm	20	51	37	94		

YARDS TO METERS
(Slightly rounded off for convenience)

yards	meters	yards	meters	yards	meters	yards	meters	yards	meters
⅛	0.15	2⅛	1.95	4⅛	3.80	6⅛	5.60	8⅛	7.45
¼	0.25	2¼	2.10	4¼	3.90	6¼	5.75	8¼	7.55
⅜	0.35	2⅜	2.20	4⅜	4.00	6⅜	5.85	8⅜	7.70
½	0.50	2½	2.30	4½	4.15	6½	5.95	8½	7.80
⅝	0.60	2⅝	2.40	4⅝	4.25	6⅝	6.10	8⅝	7.90
¾	0.70	2¾	2.55	4¾	4.35	6¾	6.20	8¾	8.00
⅞	0.80	2⅞	2.65	4⅞	4.50	6⅞	6.30	8⅞	8.15
1	0.95	3	2.75	5	4.60	7	6.40	9	8.25
1⅛	1.05	3⅛	2.90	5⅛	4.70	7⅛	6.55	9⅛	8.35
1¼	1.15	3¼	3.00	5¼	4.80	7¼	6.65	9¼	8.50
1⅜	1.30	3⅜	3.10	5⅜	4.95	7⅜	6.75	9⅜	8.60
1½	1.40	3½	3.20	5½	5.05	7½	6.90	9½	8.70
1⅝	1.50	3⅝	3.35	5⅝	5.15	7⅝	7.00	9⅝	8.80
1¾	1.60	3¾	3.45	5¾	5.30	7¾	7.10	9¾	8.95
1⅞	1.75	3⅞	3.55	5⅞	5.40	7⅞	7.20	9⅞	9.05
2	1.85	4	3.70	6	5.50	8	7.35	10	9.15

AVAILABLE FABRIC WIDTHS

25"	65cm	50"	127cm
27"	70cm	54"/56"	140cm
35"/36"	90cm	58"/60"	150cm
39"	100cm	68"/70"	175cm
44"/45"	115cm	72"	180cm
48"	122cm		

AVAILABLE ZIPPER LENGTHS

4"	10cm	10"	25cm	22"	55cm
5"	12cm	12"	30cm	24"	60cm
6"	15cm	14"	35cm	26"	65cm
7"	18cm	16"	40cm	28"	70cm
8"	20cm	18"	45cm	30"	75cm
9"	22cm	20"	50cm		

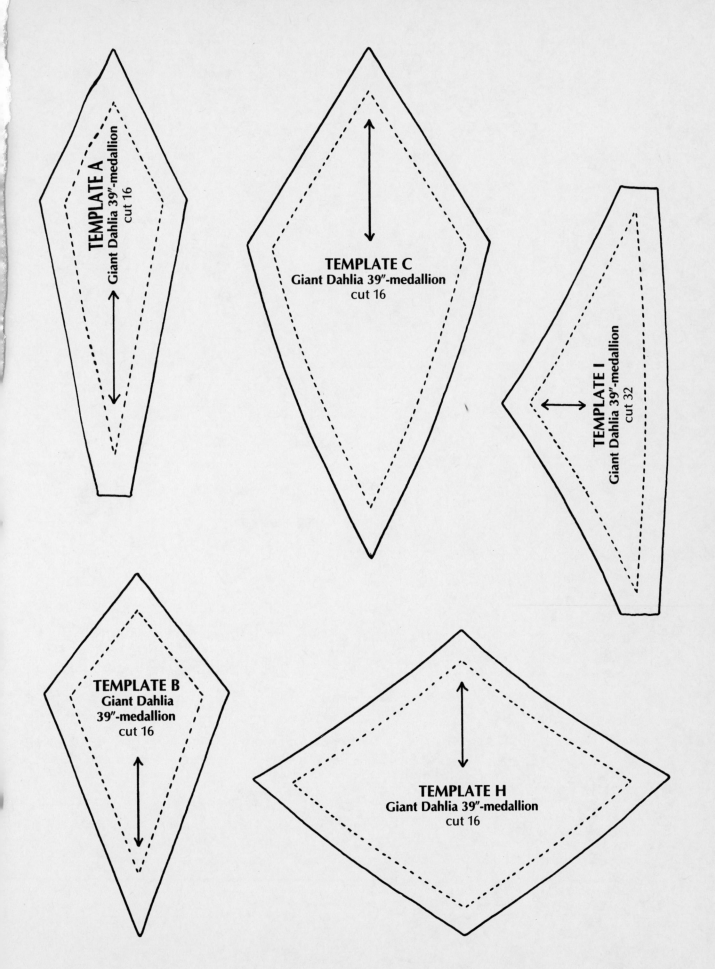

TEMPLATE A
Giant Dahlia 39″-medallion
cut 16

TEMPLATE C
Giant Dahlia 39″-medallion
cut 16

TEMPLATE I
Giant Dahlia 39″-medallion
cut 32

TEMPLATE B
Giant Dahlia
39″-medallion
cut 16

TEMPLATE H
Giant Dahlia 39″-medallion
cut 16

PLATE 1

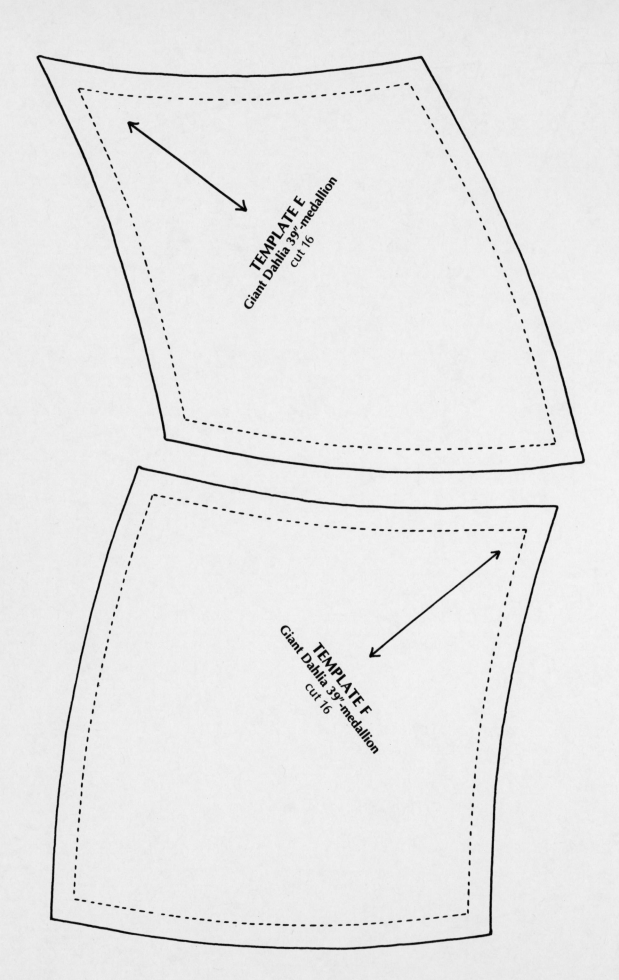

TEMPLATE E
Giant Dahlia 39"-medallion
cut 16

TEMPLATE F
Giant Dahlia 39"-medallion
cut 16

PLATE 2

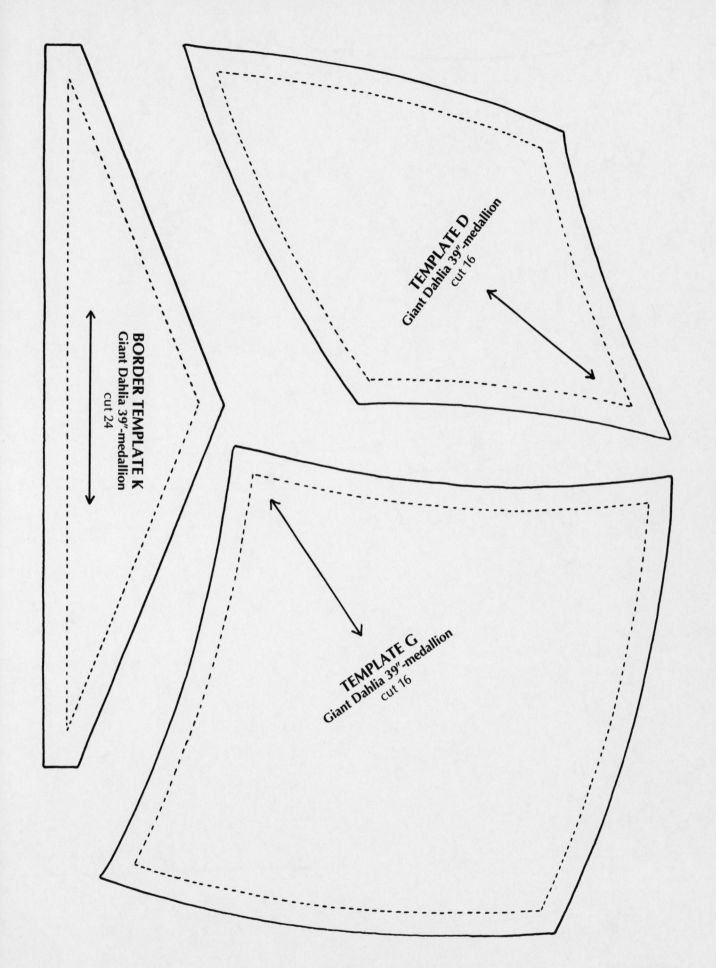

TEMPLATE D
Giant Dahlia 39"-medallion
cut 16

BORDER TEMPLATE K
Giant Dahlia 39"-medallion
cut 24

TEMPLATE G
Giant Dahlia 39"-medallion
cut 16

PLATE 3

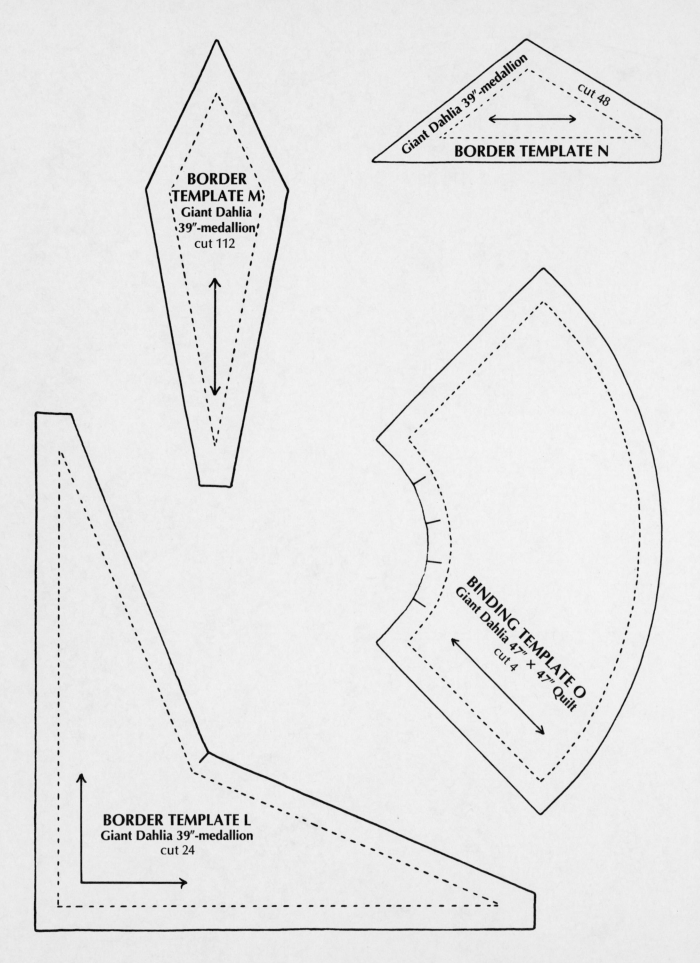

BORDER
TEMPLATE M
Giant Dahlia
39"-medallion
cut 112

Giant Dahlia 39"-medallion   cut 48
BORDER TEMPLATE N

BINDING TEMPLATE O
Giant Dahlia 47" × 47" Quilt
cut 4

BORDER TEMPLATE L
Giant Dahlia 39"-medallion
cut 24

PLATE 4

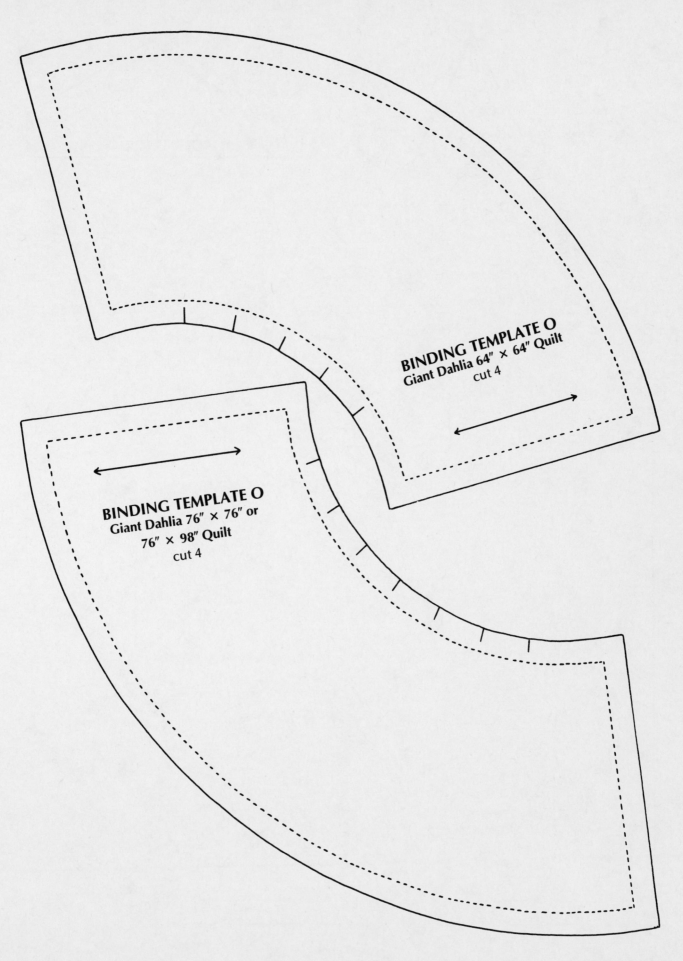

BINDING TEMPLATE O
Giant Dahlia 64" × 64" Quilt
cut 4

BINDING TEMPLATE O
Giant Dahlia 76" × 76" or
76" × 98" Quilt
cut 4

PLATE 5

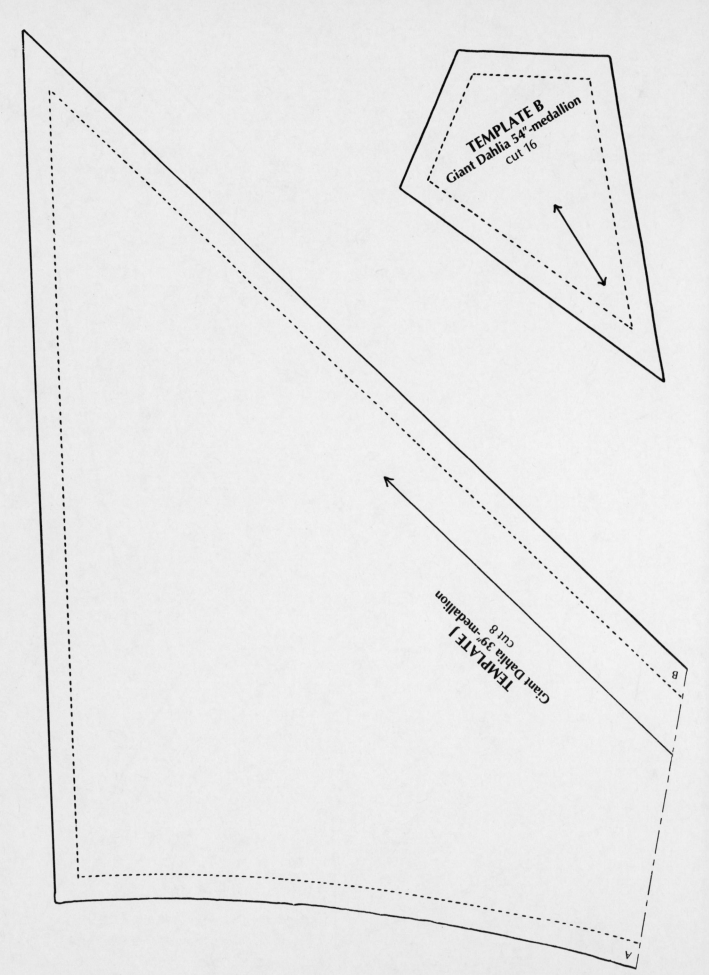

TEMPLATE B
Giant Dahlia 54"-medallion
cut 16

TEMPLATE J
Giant Dahlia 39"-medallion
cut 8

B

A

PLATE 6

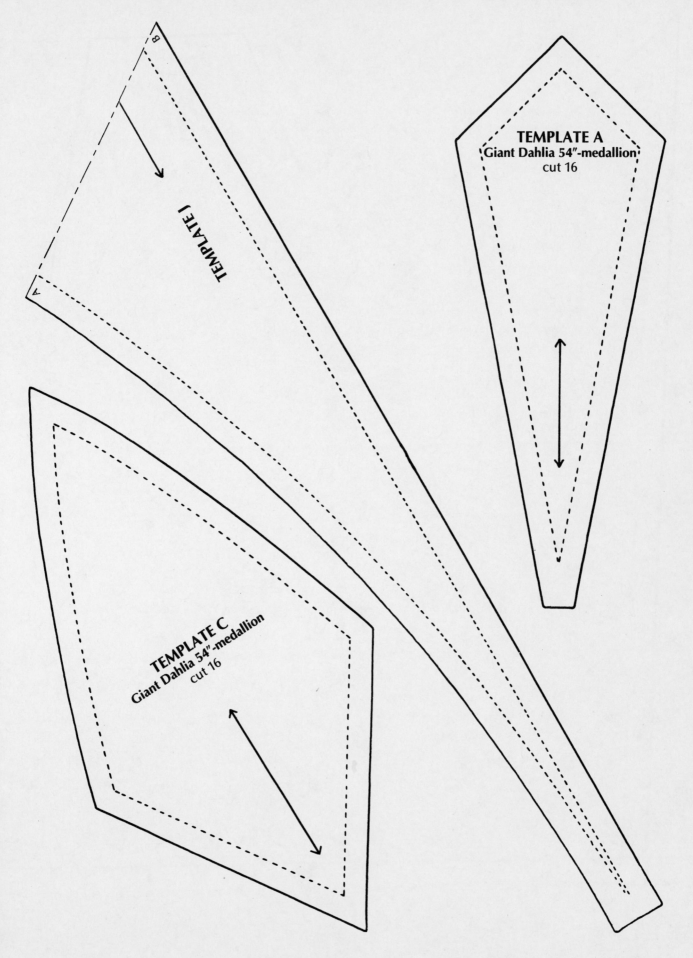

TEMPLATE A
Giant Dahlia 54"-medallion
cut 16

TEMPLATE I

TEMPLATE C
Giant Dahlia 54"-medallion
cut 16

PLATE 7

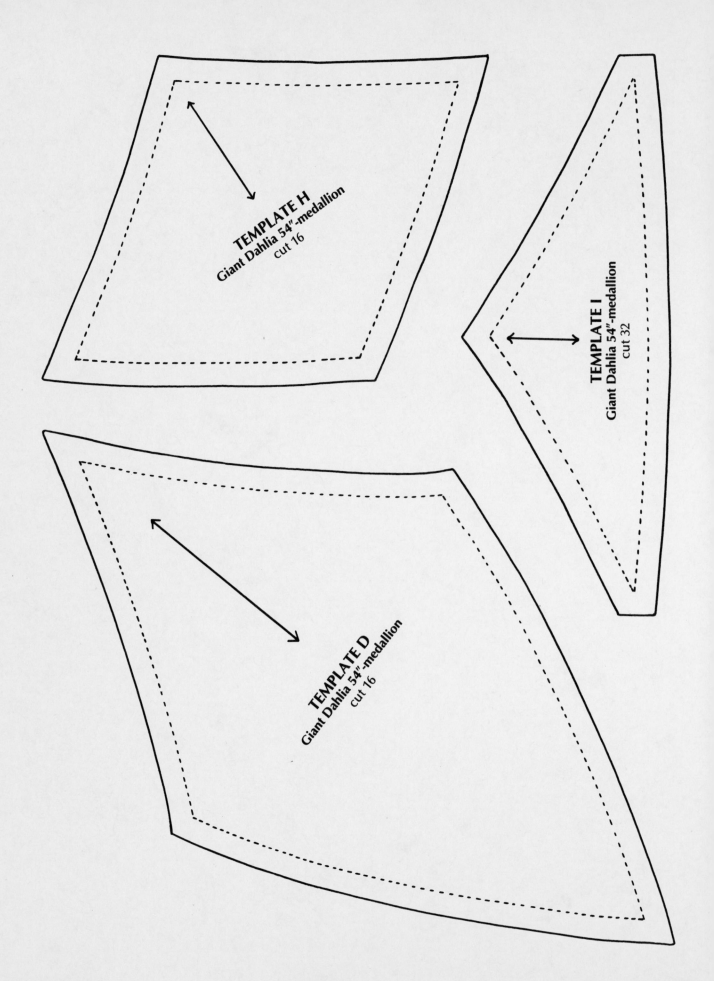

TEMPLATE H
Giant Dahlia 54"-medallion
cut 16

TEMPLATE I
Giant Dahlia 54"-medallion
cut 32

TEMPLATE D
Giant Dahlia 54"-medallion
cut 16

PLATE 8

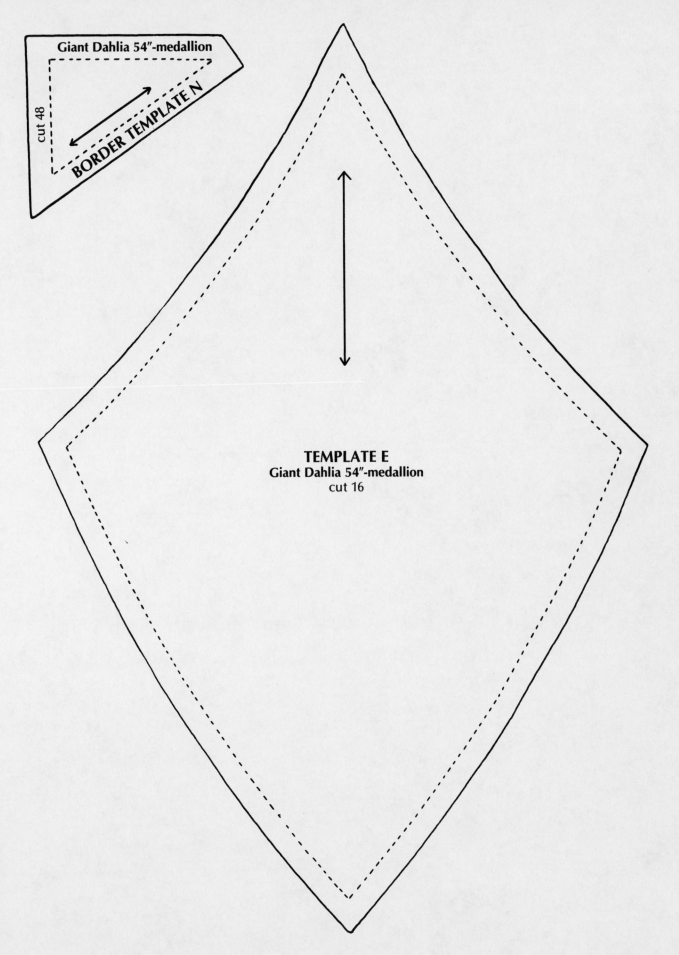

Giant Dahlia 54"-medallion

cut 48

BORDER TEMPLATE N

TEMPLATE E
Giant Dahlia 54"-medallion
cut 16

PLATE 9

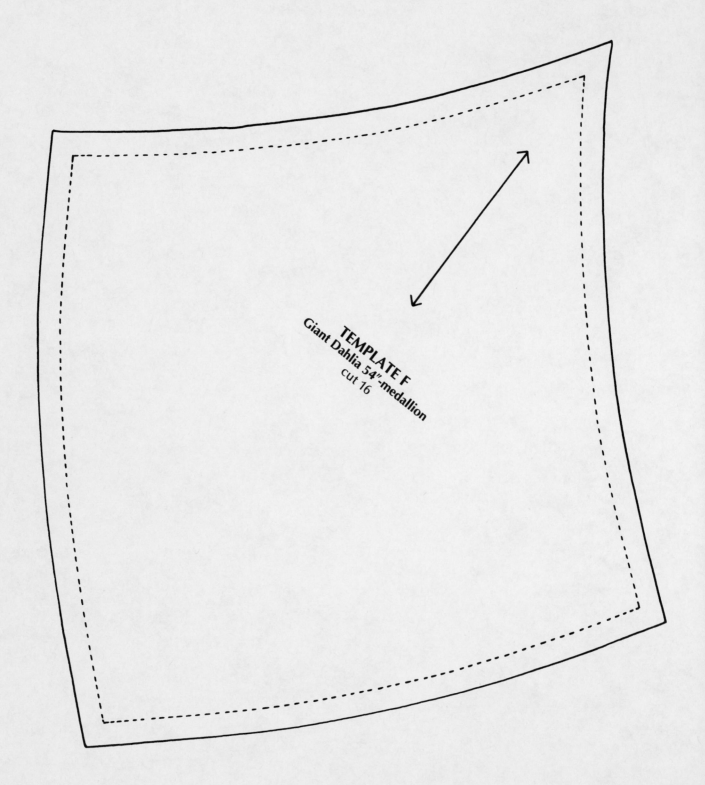

TEMPLATE F
Giant Dahlia 54"-medallion
cut 16

PLATE 10

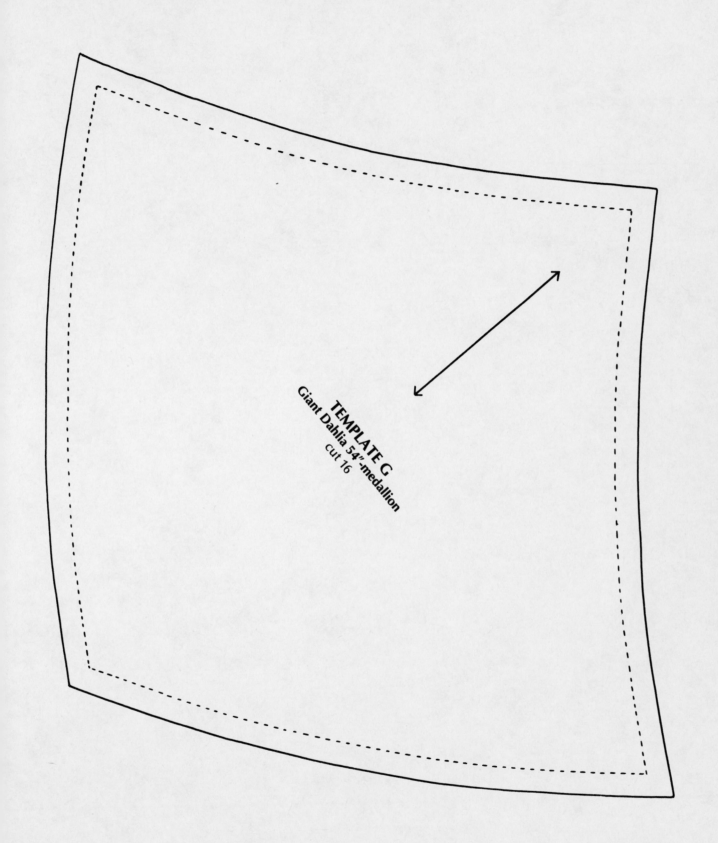

TEMPLATE G
Giant Dahlia 54"-medallion
cut 16

PLATE 11

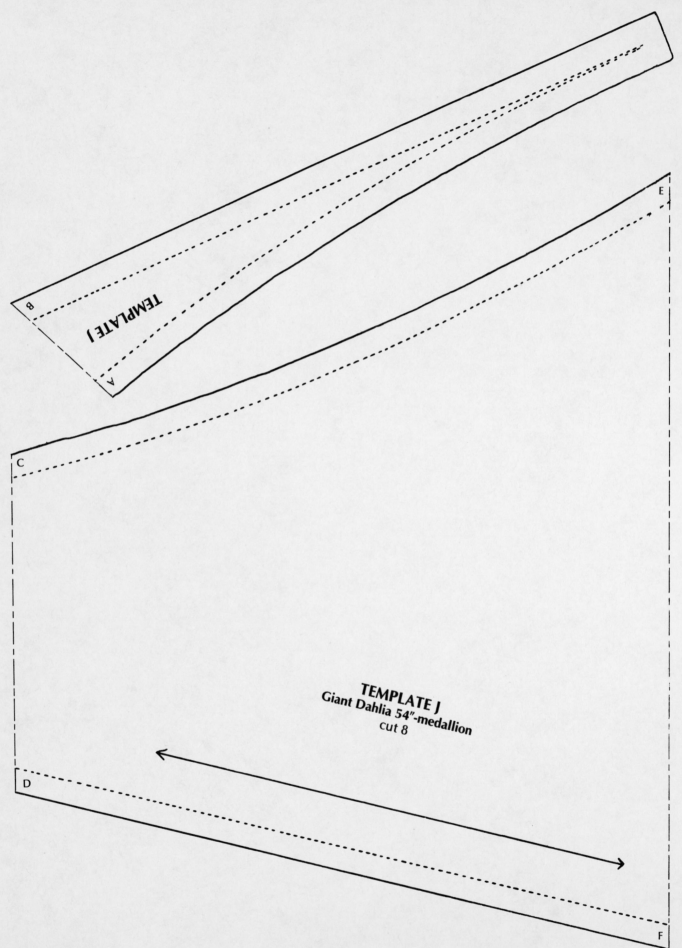

TEMPLATE J
Giant Dahlia 54"-medallion
cut 8

PLATE 12

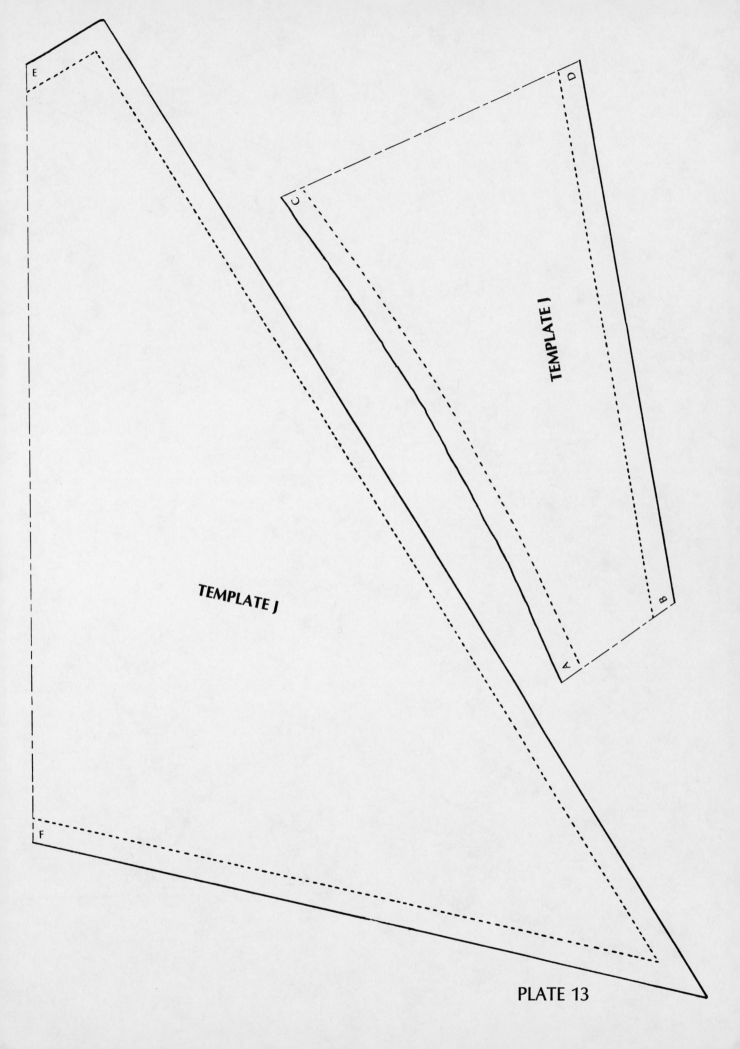

TEMPLATE J

TEMPLATE J

PLATE 13

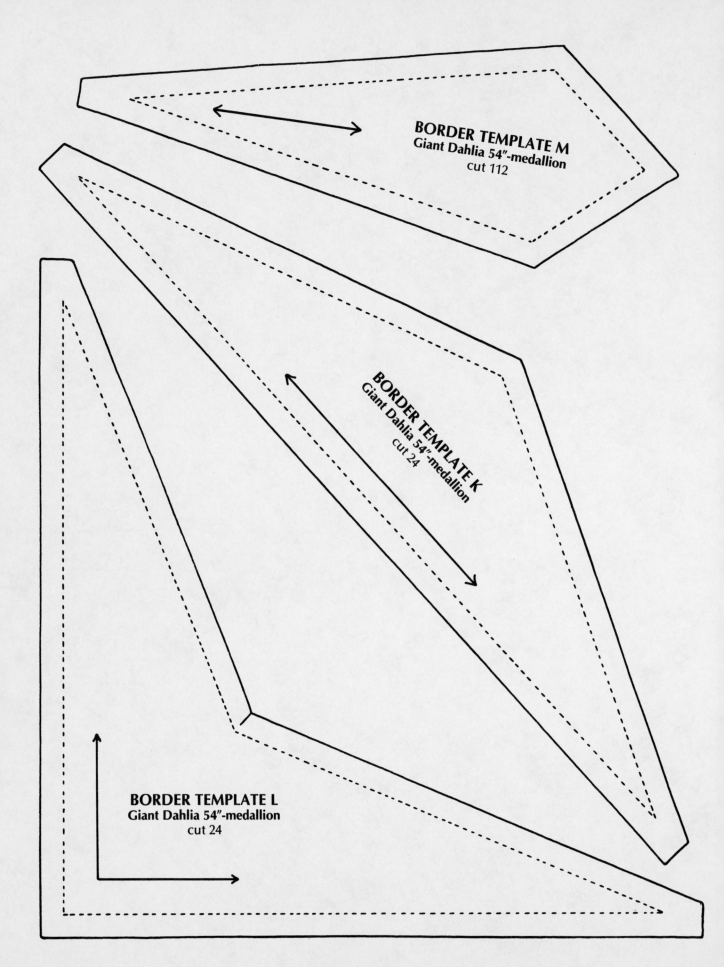

BORDER TEMPLATE M
Giant Dahlia 54"-medallion
cut 112

BORDER TEMPLATE K
Giant Dahlia 54"-medallion
cut 24

BORDER TEMPLATE L
Giant Dahlia 54"-medallion
cut 24

PLATE 14

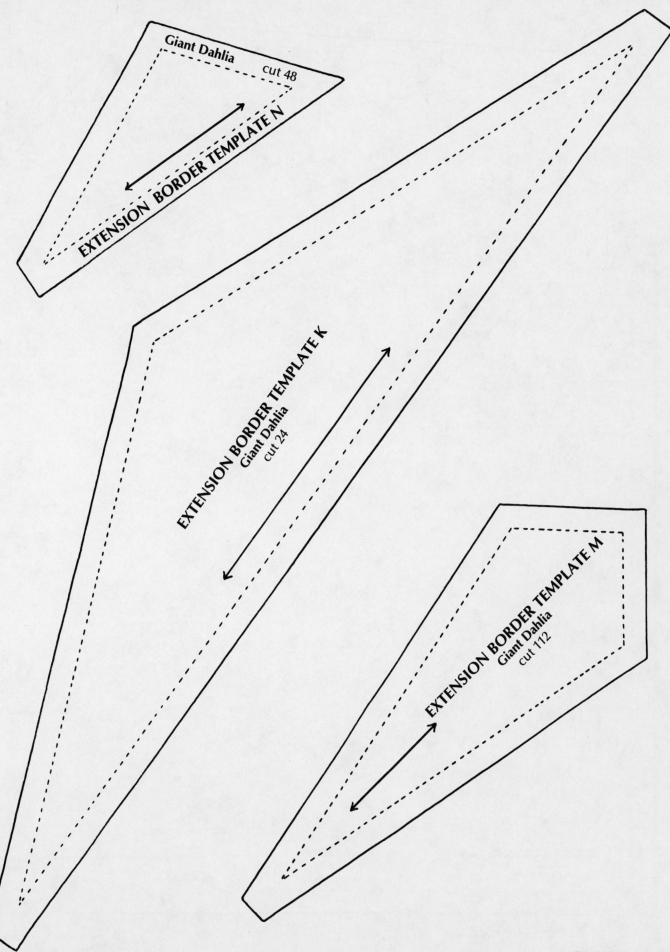

Giant Dahlia
cut 48
EXTENSION BORDER TEMPLATE N

EXTENSION BORDER TEMPLATE K
Giant Dahlia
cut 24

EXTENSION BORDER TEMPLATE M
Giant Dahlia
cut 112

PLATE 15

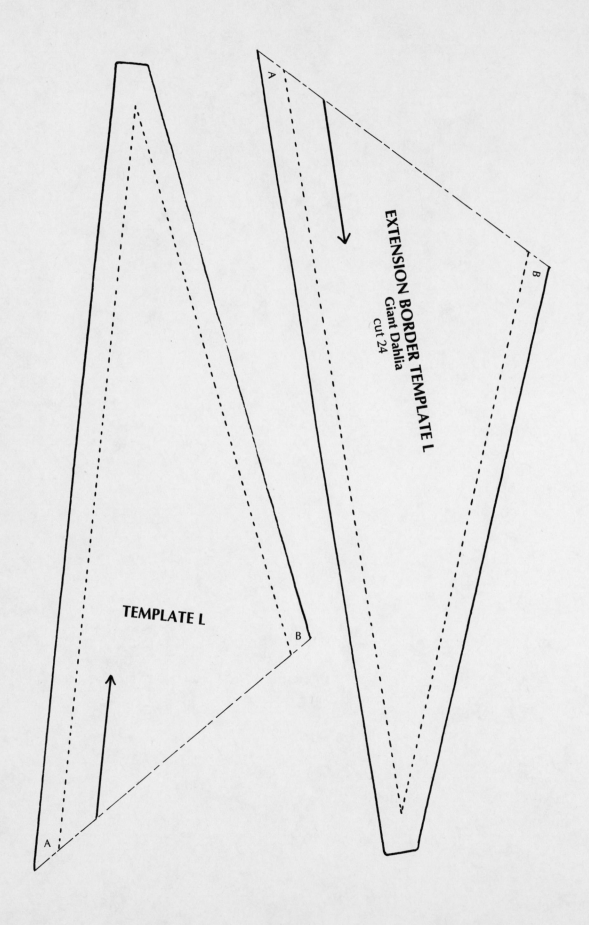

TEMPLATE L

EXTENSION BORDER TEMPLATE L
Giant Dahlia
Cut 24

PLATE 16